HRISHIKESH TAMKHANE

MY INDISPENSABLE VIEWS OF LIFE

My experiences in different areas of life

Hrishikeshtamkhane

First Published in September 2021

ISBN: 978-93-5472-036-9

BLUEROSE PUBLISHERS
www.bluerosepublishers.com
info@bluerosepublishers.com
+91 8882 898 898

Cover Design:
Nirmal K Manoj

Typographic Design:
Vaishnavi Tiwari

Distributed by: BlueRose, Amazon, Flipkart

Preface

I never thought that I would write a book. But I felt the need to share my ideas, thoughts, my thinking process, and many more things, I decided to share these things through writing a book. It took me one year to write this book. For writing this book, I conducted many kinds of research which helped me in expanding my mind and knowledge. It took many days for each and every topic of this book.

This book is mainly focused on 'self' and what it's duty towards itself and others. When you will read this book, there will be more clarity in your life. This book will bring a great change in your life.

Acknowledgement

I always believe that while doing any work, many people play an important role in our work. First and foremost, thanks to my family members - Vinod Tamkhane, Kalpana Tamkhane and Damini Tamkhane who always motivated and encouraged me. I am eternally grateful to my 'proof writer' who spent his precious time to me. He taught me many things about language, grammar and so on. I would like to express my sincere gratitude to my college friend whose support was instrumental. Finally, thanks to everyone who supported me.

Contents

IT ALL STARTS WITHIN YOU

Do you know about the biggest mystery of yourself? You may be unaware of this truth. The truth is - 'You are only you. Nothing is without 'you, you are everything and everything is within you'. But today's reality is that we don't know about it. Let's understand the above-mentioned sentence.

Everyone wants to get success in her/his life, everyone wants to be happy. Everyone wants to be great in her/his life.

To achieve a great life, to be successful in life, to become a great person etc, all these things are also within you.

Let's see these things-

- The biggest power in the world that is desire is within you.
- The potential that you need to be exceptional and exploring is already within you.
- The vision that you need to make your dream come true and illusion into reality is also within you.
- The belief which makes your body and mind strong is already within you.
- The spirit that makes you fight back is already within you.
- The happiness is already within you.

Everything is within you; nothing will be found outside.

The only thing you have to do is that you have to create an awareness about these things which are already within you.

A question can be arisen like 'When will you be aware of these things?'

If you come into contact with some people, you will understand one thing that people are stuck within their day-to-day activities. They don't have time for themselves. They always give excuses like 'I don't have time' or 'I am busy' etc. In fact, they don't focus on themselves. They spend more time in gossiping with others. By doing all these things, they don't have time for themselves. If you see these kinds of people, you will find the following things in them.

- Lack of observation
- Unstable mind
- Tiredness

So, here is the question - 'What is the way to know yourself?'

If you really want to know about yourself, then make your mind calm. The best and easiest way to make your mind calm is through meditation. When your mind is calm, you will start to observe the things which are around you, including yourself. You can be curious after observing anything. Then, you will start asking questions to yourself. Then, there will be more clarity in your life. Your understanding level will be increased. You will be able to understand so many things.

Calm mind, observation and questioning can be created with meditation.

In this way, you can be aware of your life.

Awareness is just like a light in your life. You can understand everything if the quality of your life is dependent on your awareness. If you are fully aware of your life, you will be able to control your life.

In this way, you can be aware of your own life. And when you will be aware, you will realise that as I said previously:

- Desire
- Potential
- Vision
- Spirit
- Happiness.
- Belief

All these things are within you.

Who am I? The journey to know oneself -

Who am I? This is the biggest and the most confusing question. A lot of people are looking for its answer. Whenever I asked this question to myself, I would always wonder and become unstable. I also asked my teachers. But I didn't get a proper answer for it. Then, I realised that the question is about me. Why was I asking the question to others? In fact, the question is related to my own existence. If the same question is to be asked to anyone, what will be her/his answer? She or he will answer like – 'I am a businesswoman' or 'I am a teacher' or 'I am a businessman' or 'I am a doctor' or 'I am an engineer' etc. Some people answer the question while introducing themselves such as - 'I am... ' or 'My name is... ' or 'I belong to this and that group' and so on.

If you really want to know yourself, you need to re-programme your mind. If you see in today's world, the people are stuck to the garbage in their minds. This garbage is made up of -

- Excuses
- Negative things
- Useless information
- Wrong knowledge

Today, whatever you do or act is totally based on your information which feeds in your mind. This kind of mind cannot find the answer to 'Who am I?' The information in your mind can be like this - 'I am a teacher' or 'I am a student' or 'I am successful' or 'I failed' or 'I am only made for this and that' or 'I have achieved this and that' etc.

This is all because of the conditioning of your mind.

To know yourself, you need to break this conditioning. How to break it? It can be broken when you start to ask questions to yourself and not to others. If you ask the questions, you can remove the garbage from your mind. When this kind of garbage will be removed from your mind, then ask a question - 'Who am I?' You can get the answer that you are ***a human being with infinite potentials and energy having the capacity to create anything and to do anything.***

What is meant by energy? Your every word is filled with energy, your action is itself energy, your breathing is also energy. Your vision is also energy.

Some people think that they are very small creatures in this universe. If they see with their own vision, then they will find out that this small universe is also within them.

Where does this energy go? Let's understand it -

As I said, you are a human being with infinite potential and energy. But unfortunately, today we are not using our energy to achieve our goals. But we are using our energy for getting pleasure in different kind of addictions and so on.

Let's understand this.

Addiction to Technology -

This is a very new reality. All human beings are facing it. It's true that technology fulfils our needs. Whatever we do on our regular basis is a kind of addiction. There are millions of people who are addicted to technology.

Gadgets are fantastic things in our lives. Gadgets enhance our lives in a huge way. Among these gadgets or devices, there is a small device that is our smartphone. Nowadays, smartphones are smarter than us. An amazing thing is that smartphones are made by human beings. And one more important thing is that smartphones are controlling human beings. You will be surprised after knowing that many people have access to their work in toilets. It is difficult to imagine our life without smartphones. They can make us isolated from the real world

If you are using your smartphone daily for 4 to 5 hours, it simply means that you are wasting your energy on smartphones. It takes your energy. It catches your attention. As you spend your time on your smartphone, it sucks your energy for more and more time. Your body becomes so tired. What can you do with a tired body? You can't think big, you can't do big, and you can't act big with your tired body.

On the other hand, in the history of human beings, it happened for the first time that we can talk to each other at any time and everywhere on the earth. We are flying over the clouds and we are working in space due to technology.

In this way, you are losing your energy in these things. These addictions are gaining our energy.

How it is possible to create new or to do anything new? A tired body can't do anything new.

The solution to this problem is creating awareness. If you are using your smartphone, you don't know when to stop or how much time it should be used or for which thing it should be used. Nowadays, you use different kinds of devices. But you don't know when and how to use them because you have become addicted to technology.

These addictions are taking us into darkness. So, we need the light that is 'awareness.'

What did you learn from this chapter?

WHAT IS MENTAL TOUGHNESS

What does it mean that you are a mentally tough person? First of all, you need to understand 'what is physically tough?'

Physically tough means that when you have strength, stamina and endurance, you can call yourself a physically tough person.

Now let's understand what is mentally tough? How mentally tough a person can be depended upon the problems which she/he faces in life. I have seen many people who surrender themselves when they face any problem. We should know that if there is a problem, then there must be a solution. Yes. We give up when we face a problem in our life. Most of the people stuck in problems.

Your mental toughness is dependent upon your problems in life.

- We need proper thinking in the right direction. If your thinking will be in the wrong direction, you will never find the solution. You will be stuck in the problems permanently.

Your thinking in the right direction define your mental toughness.

- I have seen many people who turn their small problems into big ones. The problems become more critical in their life. We can't say whether these people are really strong or not. But on the other hand, when you make any big problem easy, it defines your mental toughness.

How you make any big problem easy defines your mental toughness.

The above-mentioned qualities within you make you mentally tough.

We can conclude that-

- Your mental toughness is dependent upon your problems in life.
- Your thinking in the right direction define your mental toughness.
- How you make any big problem easy defines your mental toughness.

What did you learn from this chapter?

SELF-CONFIDENCE

In this world, we have a problem. The problem is very common. I think you might have heard that someone wants to do something but she/he is scared because of a lack of self-confidence.

When I talk about self-confidence, I also talk about the improvement in yourself, updating yourself and learning new things.

Here is the thin line between self-confidence and arrogance. When your self-confidence is high, you feel good and proud of yourself. On the other hand, arrogance makes you think that you are the best and the greatest in the world. So, don't let your self-confidence be converted in to arrogance.

People think that if you have self-confidence, you can do anything. To do so, you need clarity and understanding. Without these things, you can be stupid.

Let's understand with an example-

If someone told you to jump off a mountain, and you were confident at that point, would you jump? Absolutely not. Hence, there should be understanding and clarity along with self-confidence.

Let's see how you can build your self-confidence.

1. ***Understanding***

    Yes. Understanding, you should understand that no one is perfect in this world. Even you are also not perfect. When you understand that everyone has shortcomings and lacks, you will come to know that you are not less than anyone or more than anyone. You are unique.

2. *Remember the Achievements or The Good Things in Your Life*

Sometimes, in our life, we face a lot of problems, setbacks and so on. At that moment, your self-confidence can be low. One thing you need to do is to go back to your achievements and good things that you have done. When you see your achievements and the good things in your life, you will realise what you can do and how good you are. All these things will increase your self-confidence.

3. *Focus on Yourself*

You might have heard that you are the worst enemy of yourself. You are the worst enemy of yourself because you don't focus on yourself. You don't focus on your strengths. You don't focus on your positive side. Apart from this, you only focus on others' strengths. You focus on their positive side instead of your own positive side. You focus on others' weaknesses instead of your own weaknesses. So, how can you build your self-confidence? You need to focus on your strengths, weaknesses and positive sides. When you try to make better to yourself, you will become a confident person.

4. *Be a Good Person With Others.*

Be a good person in the sense that you help the needy who really need you. When your behaviour is good with others, you understand their feelings and the situation. It increases your value and you feel gratitude. And, this feeling of gratitude increases your self-confidence.

5. *Use Affirmations.*

Positive affirmations for self-confidence can be described as a positive statement about oneself. It helps to overcome negative thinking. When you repeat them, eventually you start to believe in them and you start to do all activities regarding your affirmations and many changes take place in your life.

Here are some positive affirmations that can be used.

- I am healthy.
- My mind is brilliant.
- I am the energy.
- I am unstoppable.
- I am me.
- No one can stop me.

This is how you can boost your self-confidence.

What did you learn from this chapter?

AUTOSUGGESTION

Firstly, let's understand what exactly is an auto-suggestion. It is a form of self-suggestion in which a person can guide her/his own thoughts, feelings or behaviour.

Autosuggestion is the easiest way to re-programme your subconscious mind. We all have experienced and used autosuggestions in our life. But when we use autosuggestion, we use positive statements like - 'I am great,' 'I am a champion,' and 'Only I can do this.' Apart from this, I have also seen that most of the people use negative autosuggestions like - 'I am ugly,' 'I can't do this,' 'It seems impossible', and so on. These are the exact opposite of positive emotions.

You will be surprised to know about a quote found in an ancient text that is 'the power of life and death lies in the tongue.' This simply means that words are powerful weapons that can make you as well as destroy you. That's why we should emphasize on positive.

Talk to yourself with positive sentences. When we repeat these powerful sentences in our mind, they get embedded in our subconscious mind.

When you use an auto-suggestion, it's a kind of personal growth that is used to form a new beliefs about yourself. And the most important and useful thing is that it helps to destroy bad habits.

Autosuggestion works by placing new and positive ideas in your subconscious mind and it makes us believe that it's true.

Creating Autosuggestions -

- Ensure that the autosuggestion used by you is believable. It means that you should believe in it. Then, it will surely work. If you don't believe in it, it will not ever work.
- It is a high priority to have emotions. When you talk about any kind of autosuggestion, it must be connected with your feelings.
- Autosuggestions are for ourselves not for others. Ensure that it is connected to what you want rather than others.
- Autosuggestions are very effective when they sync with your positive thinking. And, they also try to make you motivated.
- You need to repeat your autosuggestion by using more emotions.
- You need to visualize your autosuggestion so that you are acting or performing.

What did you learn from this chapter?

BECOMING UNSTOPPABLE IN LIFE

I have a question. 'What does it mean that you are unstoppable?' It means that things like others' opinion, people who gossips, others' actions, their comments, or someone quarrelling with you, don't affect you. These are external things. It doesn't mean that you are unstoppable until you become stronger from inside. At that time, these things will not affect you externally as well as internally.

Hence, there arises the question of how to become unstoppable in life. It means no one will stop you from reaching your goal and purpose in life. Let's see... .

When I talk about being unstoppable in life, there are many obstacles that stop us from becoming unstoppable. But the obstacles which I am talking about are nothing but the people and you yourself.

Let's understand this -

What about people? I have seen many people who are scared of not the people, but their opinion. 'After every action, you start questioning yourself and think that people will judge you for everything and anything you do.'

It all depends on your attitude - how you take their lies, gossips, opinions and advice.

When I was in 10th standard, I used to do different things regarding any kind of school activities. My friends used to gossip about me. They used to pass their comments on me. One day, I read a quotation - 'First they ignore you, then they laugh at you and then they fight with you, then you win.'

This thought changed my mind and made me so strong from inside.

When I talk about us as human beings, things affect us at two levels. The first level is outer and another is inner. These two layers define how unstoppable you are! Let's understand this... .

There are two voices that try to stop you from doing any work or making any decision. The voices are the people and you yourself too. The voices say things like – 'I can't do it,' 'What people will think about me,' 'What will happen, if I do this?' etc.

Whenever my friends or relatives used to gossips about me, or made me baffled with their advice and opinions, I used to do one thing. I used to listen to them. I was a good listener and had patience. So, I used to think about what they had told me; why they had told me. At last, I found that their advice and their opinions were totally useless. But at the same time, their advices indirectly helped me to become stronger from inside.

During those days, I learnt one thing that no one can stop the gossips, rumours, and so many things which people make up about you. But it totally depends on you how you take it or how they affect you.

For example – Whenever either my friends or my relatives used to give me an advice or opinion, without saying anything or being rude with them, I used to think and try to understand their advice and opinions.

'I always wondered about the reason people tell me not to do a particular work As I have noticed, most of the people who tell you to quit any work that you are doing, and they try to stop you because whatever you are doing is something they have done before. And, they have already failed in their work.

It is rare that you will see some people who try to stop you from doing any work because they have clarity and vision of your work.

That's why you should always think about others' advice and opinions. Because, there is a message hidden in every advice and opinion.

Not every advice and opinion can stop you, but some can save you.

- Hrishikesh Tamkhane

What did you learn from this chapter?

THINGS THAT YOU CAN CHANGE IN YOUR MIND.

I have two questions. What things are there in your life which you will like to change? What are those things that will bring a great change in your life and give a different direction to your life?

Let's see those things -

1. Thoughts

First of all, you should know that a thought is always a thought. It's we who categorize it as positive or negative. Only thoughts can make us happy or unhappy. Then why don't we think of good thoughts?

From where do these thoughts come? Our mind creates its own thoughts. It works like a factory.

When I was 15 years old, my parents used to go out of town. At that time, negative thoughts used to arise in my mind. The thoughts were like, 'What if an accident takes place or something bad happens to them?' These kinds of thoughts arose in my mind at that time. So, what would I do?

I used to take a deep breath and I always asked a question to myself when my parents were going out of town - why would this happen to them? There are other parents who might be going out of town. I found a solution that thoughts are just thoughts that arise in our mind. Our duty is to understand them.

People usually try to escape from their own thoughts. As you try to escape from it as much as possible, it arises in more quantities. Don't run away from your thoughts. Just try to understand them. The things will automatically be solved.

I have seen many people whose thinking towards society, people, nature and this world is negative. If these kinds of people are helped by someone else, instead of saying thanks to her or him, they think negatively such as – 'Why did she or he help me? Was there any selfishness behind her or hishelp? Maybe she or he wants something from me. No one is real in this world. There is no humanity in people.'

These kinds of thoughts are always heard from these people.

The questions are – 'Why are these people thinking like that? Why are their thoughts like that? Why they are so negative?' The reason behind this is their negative thinking.

This is happening because today, before doing any work in the early morning, we read and listen to all the negative news on the news channels and our smartphones. Hence, people think that nothing good is going on.That's why people are sad today.

Your negative thinking towards yourself, people and society is the main cause of all the problems in your life. That's why, think positive towards yourself, people, society etc. Your thoughts will start to change.

2. Beliefs

I have seen many people who say that their life is filled with negativity. They say that it's their bad luck having negative things in their life. But I would say that it happens because of anyone's belief. Your belief is created by your conditioning, isn't it?

Let's see how beliefs can change your life.

- ***I am not responsible –***

  This is the most common belief which I have seen in people. Stop blaming others for anything. Always remember that whatever happens in our life, it doesn't matter whether it is bad or good. It happens because of us.

  Someone has truthfully said that we are the biggest obstacle in our own path. Stop saying 'it's because of my boss.'

  'It's all because of my family.'

  'It's all because of my friends.'

  'It's all because of my partners.'

  And, a lot of examples are there like this –

  I have listened the most common sentence from people that bad things always happen to them. This sentence makes them weak. If you will repeat this sentence in any situation or event in your life, you will always be disconnected from society, the people around you, family, and the most common thing is that you will be disconnected from yourself.

- ***I need someone who will complete me –***

This is one of the biggest problems of people. 'I really need someone who will complete my life. I believe that someone will hold my hand even in the worst situation of my life.' I see many people who even don't try to achieve anything without others. They can't do anything until and unless others help them. They believe that their life is always incomplete without others. That's why this kind of people suffer a lot. Their sufferings are that they can't live alone or that they even can't walk alone on the path of their life.

You can love and appreciate people. But when you believe that you are nothing without them. It makes your life meaningless. Don't be attached to them. Allow yourself to be free from everyone and everything. But always remember that those who walk alone are very strong not only physically but mentally.

When I say to do anything alone, it doesn't mean that you have to isolate yourself or separate physically or mentally from them. It simply means that in our life we must be ready and be capable to do anything alone.

In the path of your life, there is always someone who stands behind you. It doesn't matter directly or indirectly. They can be your friends, family, colleagues and others. So, we have to understand this one.

'In the journey of your success, every person you meet is the next step towards your success.'

- Hrishikesh Tamkhane

➢ ***Money can do anything –***

This is the biggest problem of the people. Many people spend their whole lives chasing money because of their wrong belief. They believe that money is everything for them. But we have to understand that there is nothing wrong with making more money, earning money and getting more and more money.

But what if money makes you alone? Money takes an important place in your life. Money is not more important than your life and your family. Just think about it.

Many people get confused between time and money. According to you, what is more important – time or money? What would you choose between them?

Let's understand the difference between money and time.

See, if you have time, you can earn money again. But, if you don't have time, no matter how much money you spend, you cannot earn time again.

I have seen many people to define success to be achieved more money in life. Those people have the ultimate aim in life of making money only.

Always remember money can be a part of your life, not become your life.

3. Mindsets

There are so many mindsets that affect our happiness and many more things directly. Let's see some of them-

- ***I have no control over my life -***

  I have seen many people who always blame others for who they are, where they are and why they are. It makes them stuck. These kinds of people always stuck with their problems. That's why you should change your mindset. Most people think that they have no control over their life. But it's not true. Everyone has control over her/his life. Always look for solutions instead of looking for problems. Try to overcome, not to get stuck.

- ***I don't have the power to change -***

  Most people think very little about their life. In fact, you have great power to change yourself. You have the power to bring a great change in society. You have the power to change your situation. Every person has potential,energy, thinking power, belief system and many things.

'If you really want to bring a change, awareness and action are two important things for it.'

-Hrishikesh Tamkhane

So, these are some common things that you can change in your mind.

What did you learn from this chapter?

WHAT IS FEAR?

There is a permanent state of fear in the minds of human beings, isn't there? Sometimes the fear of success, fear of failure, fear of being insulted, fear of living alone, fear of death, fear of living without family and fear of other things take over our life. We live in fear every single day.

But, have you ever thought about whether fear is real or it's only in our mind? Let's understand this-

Yes. Fear is not reality. Fear is only in our mind. Because, nowadays human beings are disconnected from their family, the people around them, nature and most importantly, they are disconnected from present moments. They are not living in the present. You are living in your mind. Have you ever thought about fear? Your fear revolves around your future. What will happen next? Your mind revolves around your fear. Fear doesn't exist. It's just an imaginary thing.

Just think about it. Your fear is all imaginary. People, all the time, suffer while thinking about the future and the past. They think about what will happen to them or what happened with them in past. Is it right? This thing happens because you are not living in reality. You are living in your mind. Your mind is full of imagination and past memories. If we think about it rationally, both imagination and past memories do not exist. You are sometimes lost in your imagination. You are living in a non-existential world. This is the basis of your fear.

You also live with reality. What is reality? Reality is something free from everything. It may be related to the free from the thoughts; to be connected with nature, family, friends etc. If you do so, there would be no fear in your life.

Many people ask that how to overcome fear. But you cannot overcome or fight with it. Because it doesn't exist, does it? What do you have to do then?

There are two ways to destroy fear. Let's understand with an example.

You might have watched horror movies. You get scared while watching a horror scene. However, you still watch horror movies. Why do you watch or enjoy it? Because your mind knows that it's not reality. It is just the imagination of someone. Hence, you like to watch horror movies.

Normally, human beings suffer from psychological fear. People are stuck with the consequences. They think about others' opinions. What will other people think or say about them? This kind of situation creates psychological fear in them. The solution to psychological fear is nothing but to understand the things which you are doing.

Another type of fear is physical fear.

Whenever it rains heavily, lightning or thunderstorms can be seen there. In that situation, you get stuck and you are afraid of going out in the rain. So, this fear is something you must have.

There is an another example that you have worked hard for last 6 years, and you have earned a lot of money. But you don't have any fear regarding theft of your money. At that point, you are fearless. It will be your stupidity if you don't have any fear related to your money that can be stolen any time. You will have fear about the property which you have acquired with your hard work. It is good for you.

So, we can conclude that psychological fear doesn't work without understanding. On the other hand, physical fear is only proper planning, knowledge, understanding of the things which you are doing.

If you understand these things, there would be no fear.

What did you learn from this chapter?

DEVELOP A STRONG MIND.

When you develop a strong mind, you will develop a strong life. If you are strong mentally, your life becomes stronger.

How to develop a strong mind?

A person would sometimes ask me whether she or he can develop her/ his mind without taking years, months or days. But that is not possible. The truth is that no one can develop a strong mind overnight. It takes many things like -

1. ***A strong mind develops with learning new things-*** Each and every day, you have to start to learn new things. It doesn't matter whether the things are small or big. But remember, it should be new. If you look around yourself, you will find so many things which teach us something new. Observe them and try to learn something new from those things.

2. ***You take your diet to keep your body fit and healthy*** - In the same way, you also have to take a mental diet which includes -feeding your mind with positive things and reading books, especially based on failure. You must read positive thoughts every single day. When you read positive thoughts every day, the chemical named serotonin creates a feeling of well-being. After reading positive thoughts, your mind becomes more capable to solve your problems. And, it also increases the capability to think. In this way, you can read anything that is positive every single day.

3. ***A strong mind develops with a desire*** - You need a desire to make your mind strong. When you have a desire in your mind, you don't need to do anything.

Your desire will do anything to reach your destination. Thus, a desire develops a strong mindset.

4. ***Be the first*** - There are many people who are afraid to be the first in work. They also afraid of taking risks, challenges, self-improvement and knowing themselves etc. When you are the first in every situation of your life, it makes your mind strong.

5. ***Awareness*** - Awareness act like a light in one's life. The combination of awareness and focus makes your mind strong. If you are aware of your life, you understand your life in a better way.

6. ***A strong mind means to refuse to give up*** - Always remember that if you refuse to quit, miracles will happen in your life. It means you push yourself mentally and physically. It makes you good, better and best. In this way, you can develop a strong mind.

7. ***Take responsibility for your life*** - You see many people around you. Their life is controlled by others and not by themselves because they are afraid to take their own responsibility. These kinds of people have a very poor and weak mindset. If you want a strong mindset, you have to take responsibility for your life. To take responsibility for your own life is nothing but you will be responsible for things that should be done by you and not by others. It may be failure or success. You will be totally responsible for it. Taking responsibility for your life is a sign of a strong mind.

What did you learn from this chapter?

COVID-19 - THE ULTIMATE REVOLUTION.

In the history of human beings, different kind of viruses have affected human beings. A number of people died due to viruses. But this time, I think it was the biggest challenge for human beings.

Let's understand that how covid-19 became a great revolution in the history of human beings.

Human beings were going through new and unprecedented experiences because of coronavirus. There is no doubt that this virus changed the face of human society.

Have you ever heard about lockdown? It means to completely stay at home. And due to covid-19, many affected countries decided to declare lockdown in their countries.

In the period of lockdown, there has been an increase in domestic violence cases ana suicides, many people lost their jobs, there was a lack of supply of basic needs and a number of people stuck to the work location. Many people who had arrived in the city migrated to their villages on foot. So many people died of the looming fear of hunger. Women, men and children were forced to begin the arduous journey of going back to their villages by cycling or hitching a ride on trucks, lorries, water tanker and milk vans.

Some of the migrant people had children who were migrating from one place to another. There were some pregnant women who gave birth to their babies on the road. In this situation, many people showed sympathy for the needy. ***They showed their humanity.***

Those who were at home suffered from mental health issues like stress, anxiety, overthinking and a lot of people were suffering from loneliness. Few of them committed suicide.

The lockdown impacted three main areas like physical movement, social distance and restricted availability of the most public services.

You saw the impact of covid-19 on human beings. But what about birds, animals and plants?

Let's see what happened with nature.

Surprisingly, there were some good effects on nature due to the lockdown. They are given below.

- Decrease in air pollution.
- Reduction of noise pollution.
- Immaculate beaches.
- Amazement to see animals.
- The emergence of wild animals on the streets of urban areas.
- The peaceful atmosphere of the city.
- Urban areas attracted the animals.
- The sky was crystal clear.
- The air was fresh.

During the lockdown, people were completely staying in their houses. Because of this, the people were suffering from anxiety, fear, and stress. Social media has played a very important role in spreading awareness and knowledge among the people. But at the same time, it has also been misused for spreading fake news, fake videos and fake information. During the pandemic, the social media panic spread faster than the covid-19 virus.

My personal experience during lockdown -

I, as a motivational speaker, sometimes think about how I can teach people in a way that will affect them. It will help them to learn faster. But this situation taught us so many things that I would not have considered before when trying to teach people.

As we are connected to each other, we need to save our earth. We also need to take care of our health. These things are not taken seriously by the people. As I said, human beings are in exploitive mode. Being human beings, we have forgotten about nature, it's beauty,it's value and importance.

Let's see what I learnt during this pandemic-

I learnt to help others in difficult situation. I suffered mentally more than physically because the quarantine centre was beside my home. The animals were seen on the streets, the birds were flying fearlessly. When I saw them, they were just enjoying their freedom in this world.

I have heard that the safest place is your home. I really realised it at that time.

I am a student of psychology. So, I knew the importance of mental health.

It seemed that nature was recovering. Because everything was stopped due to lockdown.

I still remember when the patient of the coronavirus was brought to the quarantine centre which was beside my home. It was striking 12 o'clock at night. I could clearly see the stress on his face.

It will take time to make everything okay.

I knew the importance of health in real way – 'Health is the real wealth.'

I knew the importance of a healthy lifestyle. Whenever I used to see patients beside my home, I would experience the fear of death.

During the lockdown period, I learnt a lot of things. I did new things. As time went by, the fear of the virus was also decreasing.

I made new friends in my area. Because it was not possible to go out, I spent more time in playing, laughing and so on. It was a daily routine of mine to spend more time with my friends. One thing, I also learnt to do something in life, one needs not be alone physically but mentally.

In this way, it was an unprecedented experience for everyone.

What did you learn from this chapter?

WAR BETWEEN HUMAN BEINGS AND NATURE

The earth is a fantastic and amazing planet. Billions of creatures live on it. Every creature has unique features and characteristics. Some creatures cannot be seen with our eyes, some creatures live in water, some of them can live in water as well as on land – we call them amphibians. We also find a variety of plants, animals, insects etc. This is a mind-blowing thing about our planet.

As far as my opinion is concerned, we have exploited the land, exploited the oceans. Our idea of life has become exploitation. We as human beings have killed a large number of animals.

Everyone wants more and more, everyone wants to expand more after seeing all these things. Today's human being has become an exploitive mode.

As the human beings, we are the most powerful creatures on the earth. Because on this earth, human is the creature who has made changes in himself since ancient times. And these changes are accepted by nature.

Once upon a time, human beings were totally dependent on nature. And, we have already studied how human beings were dependent on nature. To depend on nature means to include natural things in eating, living, and drinking. In today's livelihood, human beings include those natural things very rarely.

If we go back to our past, we used to live together. We used to share our problems with each other. Today, we do the same things. But those things are to be done very rarely by us. In today's world, though we are living together, we have some shortcomings.

We can see progress in each and every field. But with the progress, we have created many serious problems for us.

According to me, development is essential. As I said previously, gadgets make our life easy. It is good for human beings. But while developing, we have created great problems not only for ourselves but for the planet earth.

The most important thing is that we live in the world of the internet. Because of misuse of the internet, human beings have been facing very serious issues. It is not really good for human beings. So, we can conclude that -

Today, this is the biggest war between human beings and nature.

Let's understand this statement.

We are able to think and imagine. We have emotions. We have developed our body which is able to do any work in this world. It doesn't matter whether human beings are working on the earth or in space. As human beings, we have some unique characteristics and technologies. Anything is possible for human beings. There are some tools which make our life luxurious. New researches are to be conducted in the world. But what about nature? Though we have developed lots of things in this world, is it good for nature? Is it good for animals and birds? Is it good for our planet?

Development is good as long as it harms nothing. But if it starts to harm, it's not called as the development. It's known as the destruction.

Nowadays, global warming is increasing consequently. We are polluting everything. We are destroying our nature by throwing plastic in to society. One more tragic thing is that people throw plastic in the river, seas, and oceans. It affects aquatic life. We should know that 70% of life is underwater.

The way we are living, the way we are finding our food, the way we are making our clothes, accessories and other things made up with leather (skin of animals). All these things are used by human beings. Due to this, many species on the earth are on the brink of extinction. This shows the tendency and vision of human beings towards nature.

The earth is in danger because of humans' stupidity and greedy nature. We need to think about nature.

So, basically, today's biggest war is between human beings and nature. As I said human being is on exploitive mode. The solution to this kind of war is human awareness and intelligence towards nature and themselves.

What did you learn from this chapter?

COMMON REGRETS IN LIFE

If I ask you, 'What is the worst feeling in the world or our life?' it is possible that you probably don't know the answer to this question. If you ask this question to any old person, he can tell you about the worst feeling in the world.

There is my granny's home nearby my home. I have a habit of spending one and a half hour with her in the evening. One day I was missing my friends as usual in the evening. I went to my granny. I asked her about her friends. I asked her about where her friends were and how they were. She became emotional after listening my questions. Then, she started to tell me about her friends. When I asked her when she had met them last time, the way she looked at me, her eyes were full of sorrow. At that time, I could see the feeling of regret in her eyes. She said that she couldn't meet her old friends for a long time. Even, she didn't know where they were or they are alive or dead.

On that day, I realized that there is no worse feeling than regret. Hence, I decided to share some common regrets of our life.

1. ***I wish I had taken a risk in my life –***

   I have seen many people who miss an opportunity in their lives because they don't take a risk. Don't be afraid of taking a risk in your life. We just think, 'What will happen, If I do it? What will happen if I fail?' Most people don't take any risks. So, they remain an average person. Hence, take a risk if you want to grow.

2. ***I wish I remained in touch with my friends -***

   Yes, friends. A very stupid, fun, happier, sorrowful, surprising, and relaxing part of our life is a 'friend'. A friend is one who stands for us in every situation. She/he knows that what you have done for getting the things in life. She/he knows your struggle. She/he knows when you are happy and sad. Your friend is your partner in every mistake and problem. That is the only person who knows about your love and crush. We share everything with our friends as we can't share those things with our family members, especially in the phase of puberty.

3. ***I wish I had the courage to live life according to myself -***

I think this is the most common regret of all people. Many people don't take responsibility for their life. They act like others act. They do what others do. They speak what others speak. They don't even create their own path. They always follow others' path. Always remember: be yourself. Make your own path. Take your own decisions. Don't care about it. Just remember what will happen. There are two possibilities of doing anything - The first one is that you will fail and another is that you will success. Apart from these two, nothing will happen to you.

And, what is the matter if you fail? No one will throw you out of this world. Always remember that failure is necessary in our life. Because when you fail, you learn something. You become strong from the inside. But always remember one thing that you should make your own choice and your own decisions. Because only you know what is right and wrong for you.

4. *I wish I had time to spend with my family -*

This is also one of the most common regrets of the people. In fact, nowadays, this regret is found in all the youngsters.

We should know that everyone has to work, everyone has to earn money. Everyone has to make her/his dream come true. But we should also know what is more important for us. Yes, it's our family who we work for very hard to get this and that. But we forget why we earn money, why we work hard. These things revolve around our family. We also forget to spend time with our family. Spend more and more time with your family. Your time is the most precious gift for your family.

We mess up many things in our family. Sometimes, after getting busy, we forget our family members. We don't have the time to know our family members. We never try to understand our family members. We don't even know what they like and what they don't like. In this way, we mess up so many things. That's why you should spend more and more time with your family.

5. *It's never too late -*

Yes, really, it's never too late to begin new. It's never too late to make a decision. It's never too late to reinvent yourself. It's never too late to learn something new. It's never too late to start something. It's never too late to grow. It's never too late to enjoy. It's never too late to do something great in our life. It's never too late to learn. It's never too late to live a new life. It's never too late to change our thoughts. It's never too late to be best. Remember it's never too late to confess your love.

As human beings, we have divided our life. We also act like that. Yes, I have seen a lot of people who say that it's too late. They have some excuses like – 'Now I am tired because of my age.' Age is the main factor that I have seen. In fact, people act according to their age.

Old people always judge themselves on the basis of their age. If you ask any old person to play with you, he will absolutely say that it's not his time to play. His time has gone. But the reality is that it's never too late. So, start where you are, because, it's never too late to do anything.

We are all same at the last breath of life.

-Hrishikesh Tamkhane

What did you learn from this chapter?

THE PERFECT WAY TO START AND END YOUR DAY

How to start and end our day is an important aspect that plays a vital role in being successful.

Hence, the first thing you have to do after waking up is to say 'thanks' to yourself. Now it's a new day for you. A new day means everything new.

A new day brings -

- New challenges
- New opportunities
- New hope comes with a new day
- New problems that make you strong
- New relationships that teach you mortality and values.
- New experiences

Always remember every new day in your life is the new start of your life. Be grateful for this thing.

What happens when you are grateful for what you have? Your attention goes on blessings instead of problems. And you feel positive, energetic and blessed.

Start your day with a set of intentions –

An intention is not only for you but also for others. Today, whatever you are going to do, just give your best to it. Whatever you do, just do it with perfection. If needy people want your help, help them. Everyone in this world is struggling for money, food, and other things. Today, most people are sad. You have to show some sympathy to them. You have to live in the present moment. And the most important thing is that you have to learn and teach new things.

The next thing you have to do is exercise –

The most important and essential thing to get success in your life is 'exercise.' Your body should be fit physically to work hard. An obstacle in the path of yours is laziness. Why do people live with laziness? There are many reasons behind it, but the reason which I am talking about is the lack of blood circulation in one's body. So, it is very important to exercise. Daily exercise leads to proper blood circulation in the body.

You have to remember to exercise daily if you want to go further in your life. Exercise must be done for 20 to 30 minutes.

Meditation –

When you meditate your mind becomes calm. And when your mind becomes calm, new thoughts and ideas arise in your mind. When you understand these ideas and thoughts, you start to think about them and work on them. New concepts and new innovation can be created with meditation.

This is how new concepts and innovations should be held.

The next thing you have to do is – In at early morning, your mind is always fresh and calm. So,

- Read
- Watch
- Listen

This can be positive, creative and constructive. And it can be the best food for your mind. One thing is always stated about our mind that whatever we see, listen and read whether it is positive or negative, can be seen through our actions.

Thus, you can start your day...

After doing all these things, we are going to see how to end our day or the way to end it perfectly.

Do you know, every morning comes up with challenges, opportunities and every evening ends with experiences?

Before going to bed, what do you have to do? You should analyse and summarise your day by questioning yourself.

The questions you may ask –

- What did I do today?
- Did I learn new things?
- Which things did I learn?
- Did I help someone who has come across to me?
- Whom did I meet today?

After asking the above questions to yourself, you can analyse and summarise your day.

Then, you have to plan for the next day. A new day should be started with your plan. You should think about what you have to do and what you don't have to do.

We must have a reason for getting up early in the morning.

What did you learn from this chapter?

POWER OF VISION

As human beings, we possess many powers. The power of vision is one of them. How do you see your own problems? How do you see any situation? Where you see your own position? These are the things that define your energy.

Everyone faces problems, setbacks, and failure in her/his life. There are some people who instantly overcome it. And some people are still stuck with it. So, here are the questions- Why does it happen? Why don't they overcome? The answer is very simple. It's all about their vision through which they see things.

If you don't have a vision, your mind will be stuck with the garbage only.

If you don't have any vision in your life, your life will be limited. You will not able to go beyond your limitations, possibilities and potential.

When you have a vision, you have a very clear direction of life. At that time, you don't wonder, you just focus on particular things. What do you want from your life? What do you want to do in your life? How will you do it? It's all impossible until and unless you have a vision.

There are many people who have no vision in their life. But if you don't have a vision, your life will have less energy and excitement.

When you live your life, you have a different vision in different areas of life.

Let's understand this –

- Vision for yourself - to become a good student, intellectual, intelligent, leader, ideal for everyone, inspiration for everyone.
- Family - a good family member, obedient, ideal.
- Friends - loyal, humorous, helping nature, kind.
- Social life - kind-hearted, contribution in the life of needy, helping nature.
- Physical health - do daily exercise, yoga, having a good meal, having a balance in your diet.
- Mental health - reading books, talking with intelligent people, watching any programme based on learning.
- Career - to give the best performance, trying to achieve the next position.

The research is clear. Those who have a vision about their dreams and goals will be far more successful than those who don't have a vision.

According to research, those who have a written statement of vision do much better than those who simply carry ideas around their mind. Some people always review their written visions on a daily basis. They become more successful in life.

That's why you should make your vision statement accessible. Keep a copy beside you whenever you are in your room, your office or in your workplace or wherever it is possible. The simplest way is to put it on your smartphone. You can read your vision anytime, anywhere. And you will be more aware of your vision.

Vision for your goals -

The power of vision plays a very important role in your goals. Before achieving your goal, you have to walk on the path which can lead you to your destination - it is nothing but your goal. But while walking on the path, if you have no clear vision of how you will achieve your goal, it will be impossible to walk on the path. When you face any obstacle, setback and so on, you start to enjoy it because you know that on the path that is not easy to walk, there can be many obstacles and problems. You may know the path which you have selected is very long. You may know that sometimes you will break down. You may know that it's difficult to deal with every situation. The power of vision will make you understand why this happened and why that is happening.

Vision for yourself -

Vision for yourself means - How do you see yourself? What do you think about yourself? Is there a limitation on you? What is your opinion about yourself? What do you like most about yourself? How do you think, see or feel about yourself? Because ,the way you see yourself, that kind of energy releases within you.

I have seen many people whose self-image is very low in their own vision. They always try to find some negative things in themselves. So, what kind of energy will release into them.

This is how the power of vision in different areas in your life and for yourself is!

What did you learn from this chapter?

PLANTING A DESIRE

If I ask about what the most effective power in the world is, your answers will be different. But my answer is the power of desire. Today, everyone is chasing her/his dream. Everyone is doing or trying something to achieve something only because of desire.

Just think for a moment. If there was no desire, what would happen? The lives of people will be meaningless. Everything will be useless. The power of desire is incredible. We can't imagine it.

Always remember, your desire defines your thoughts, actions, confidence, success and your life.

Many people think that they want to do a lot of things for the needy. They want to contribute something to their lives. They have a wish to do something for nature. But when will this happen? This will definitely happen when you think that you have to do something or you have to be someone in your life. You not only want to do things for yourself but also for those who are in need of you. When you think like this, a desire arises in your mind. At that moment, you need not to do anything. The desire which has arisen in your mind will make you do anything, regardless of whatever you have to do.

We must keep in our mind that this kind of desire raises thoughts, energy, confidence, struggle, action, and a feeling of achievement.

Desire = Thoughts = Confidence = Energy = Action = Struggle = Achievement.

The quality of your achievement totally depends on your desire.

So, choose a desire that will make you think about yourself and others.

What does it mean to choose a desire? The simple meaning of this is that whatever you are in the present condition or whatever you want to be in your future, maybe a businesswoman, a doctor, an engineer or a businessman etc, you should share it. It can be your good thought, it can be your help, it can be your sympathy, it can be your money, it can be your happiness, it can be your love. It can be anything.

What did you learn from this chapter?

WHAT EXACTLY IS FAILURE?

Yes, it is one of the biggest question that I have ever heard. What is failure? For many people failure is nothing. And, there are some people for whom failure is everything.

Let's understand this -

When I was in 12th standard there was my senior who was really a brilliant student. Whenever I used to ask him about his studies and the things related to his brilliance, he used to answer that his parents, friends, relatives believe that he would definitely do something great in life. On that day, I came to know that he was not studying for himself, but for his family, friends, relatives etc. He was under the expectations.

When the result was announced, he passed with average marks. His marks were good. But the burden of the expectations was more than the marks that he acquired in the exam. That's why he committed suicide and ended his life.

On that day, I knew that he was not studying for himself. But he was just studying to complete the expectations of others. His competition was only with the expectations.

What did I learn from that?

Failure is not a big thing that would lead anyone to commit suicide. But one thing that comes up with failure is the conditioning which is responsible for his suicidal attempt.

Why is failure a big thing today? Our conditioning is responsible for causing a big failure in life. Since, our childhood days, the people around us make us believe that success is more important than failure.

Both success and failure are important for life. But people have made them separate from each other. This kind of thinking of the people is passing from generation to generation. Because of that, this little thing is becoming big day by day.

You might have experienced one thing that during our childhood days, we used to do anything fearlessly. There was no boundary for us. But as we grew up, our parents as well as the people around us started to teach us to be careful before doing anything. Many people force a school or college-going student that she/he has to pass the exam. 'There is no another chance in life.' Like this, a lot of sentences are used by the people. But these kinds of sentences create fear in our mind.

I still remember when I was a child. While learning a bicycle, I fell down many times. But at the same time, I used to stand up and finally I learnt to ride a bicycle. But after growing up, we don't even try to do things again after failing once.

Just think about it and ask yourself whether a failure is really a big thing or you made it a bigger one. The answer is absolutely not.

Once you break the conditioning related to failure in your mind, you will understand that it's as important as success.

Failure is your conditioning. Once you break it, you will win.

-Hrishikesh Tamkhane

What did you learn from this chapter?

SELF-LOVE

What is self-love? A number of people do not understand 'self- love'. They think that self-love is a kind of freedom from everything that they don't like; that they can do whatever they like.

If you love your mind and body, we can call it self-love. In simple words, self-love is nothing but taking care of your body and mind. But if you are using your body only for getting pleasure like watching excessive porn videos or films, drinking alcohol, excessive use of smartphones, all these things make you addicted, if you are addicted to technology, it is not self-love. It means that you are not in love with yourself.

We can conclude that self-love is nothing but self-discipline.

A lot of people do something great in their lives. It doesn't matter at which level you will find the quality of self-discipline.

You know the greatest satisfaction is associated with people who love themselves. When you love yourself, you love or appreciate your own life.

When you love yourself, it improves your self-esteem. It boosts your confidence. But a question has arisen in my mind. What is love? Love is a feeling and action. For example, you work hard for the nourishment of your family. It is your love towards your family. Your love is expressed through your actions. Only actions define your love for others and for yourself.

When a mother feeds her baby, normally it can be noticed how nicely she feeds a baby.

On the other hand, there are some people who only have intense and burning sexual desire. They call it love. But it is not loving, merely a kind of lust.

There are two ways to love yourself.

1. Awareness -

   As I said previously, you are aware of what you want from your life, what you want to do in your life, what your potential is and what your weaknesses are. Until and unless you are aware of yourself, you can't love yourself.

2. Self-acceptance -

   When you accept yourself, you will see many changes in your life. Those who have achieved great things in their lives never think about their insecurities, their disabilities, their caste or religion. But your journey of self-love depends on your self-acceptance.

   If you want to love others, you need to love yourself first. Along with this, you need to take care of yourself if you want to care for others. If you want to do something for others, you need to do something for yourself. If you can help yourself, then you can help other people.

So, we can conclude that to work and be cautious of your body and mind, you need self-discipline. And self-discipline leads to self-love.

What did you learn from this chapter?

THE POWER OF SILENCE

In today's world, being silent is very difficult. 'Silence' is the solution to every problem in everyone's life. Silence is the first step for inner transformation.

When you are silent, you can feel everything internally. You can feel the happiness. You can feel the determination within you. You might have noticed that whatever some people say becomes true because of the silence within them. These kinds of people have a very calm mind. Whatever they do, they do it with focus.

After being silent, you can observe everything around you. Then, you can observe yourself. Different kinds of questions arise in your mind. Those questions can transform your life.

Talking with people connects us with others. But silence connects us with ourselves. A lot of people have lost themselves completely in technology.

Today we are suffering from different kinds of diseases and mental health issues.

Nowadays, depression is common among people. Your disturbed mind is the root cause of any depression. People are lost in their own thoughts. Even they don't know how to escape from their own thoughts. A silence within you can help you to escape from your own thoughts.

As I said, when you become silent, you connect yourself from inside. After being connected with yourself, you start to understand your thoughts, emotions, feelings. You also start to understand others. Once you understand yourself from the inside, then you understand others' feelings, emotions and thoughts. This quality makes you a powerful human being.

Silence is not about the absence of sound and noise. It is about pausing or taking a break from life. To enjoy yourself is to think about yourself, to enjoy the present moment.

I have seen many people to underestimate the power of silence. But the power of silence can handle any critical situation in your life. It can overcome your anger. Only silence can control your anger. You become cool. The power of silence can end all the negative thoughts. Silence can build trust, which is essential for a relationship. It's clear that silence has some power. But there are some misconceptions about silence. People think that silence is related to loneliness and isolation. But it's not true. In fact, it connects with others. It expresses what you mean really. It builds better relationships in your life.

Silence makes us to be able to understand non-verbal communication. It makes us to learn more about the people, nature and so many things.

When you are silent, you like to listen more naturally. That's why a giver tries to give you more and it enhances the relationship. For example, in the classroom, when students listen silently, the teacher also teaches effectively. She/he tries to give more to the students. It develops a good relationship between a teacher and students.

This is the power of silence.

Let's see how to embrace the power of silence.

We all know very well that many people start their day with external noise. When people get up, it is because of their alarm clocks. Many people like to listen music in toilets and bathroom. It has become a common thing among people.

We live our life full of noise. Silence is just like an opportunity for you to feel silence within you.

It seems so difficult to create silence among us. Especially in today's world, where we all are surrounded by noise. We feel uneasy while living this kind of life. We feel disturbance when there is a sudden stop in our lives. We try to avoid doing some activities in silence.

I have seen many people who have fear about silence. They are afraid to live in silence. Because according to them being alone means silence. But it's not true. Silence makes you stronger from inside.

Have you ever wondered when thoughts come into your mind? They come into your mind when you are silent.

When people live in silence, many thoughts arise in their minds. When thoughts have arisen, we try to eliminate them rather than understand them. When you understand your own thoughts, your understanding level increases and you become stronger from inside. Thus, silence makes you stronger.

What did you learn from this chapter?

WHAT IS DEATH?

It is the question, isn't it? So many of you are looking for the answer to this question.

When I was in 12th standard, this question was wandering in my mind all the time. Even now, while writing this book, this question makes me so demotivated. It's a great struggle with this question.

Sometimes, I used to forget the question regarding death whenever I was with my friends, family, relatives etc. But whenever I was alone, the same question made me confused and I used to be demotivated, unfocused and tired all the time.

One day, I decided to ask the question to my teacher. My teacher tried to answer my question. He tried to make me understand what he said. But it wasn't sufficient. Still, the struggling was going on with the question.

As I was struggling with this question at some point, I had decided to give up my work, my study, motivational speaking and many more things.

I didn't do any work for 5 or 6 days. I was just spending more time doing regular activities like bathing, watching TV, sleeping and repeated all the activities again and again.

I was just thinking that -

We take birth. Then we struggle to live. Somehow, we get an education, we learn new things. We enjoy, we help the needy, we fall in love, we motivate, or inspire ourselves and others, we fall down and rise back up. Then we become successful after doing all these things at a particular age.

But have you ever thought about what the last destination of your life is? The answer is death.

Yes, I try to understand death. So, my journey started from here to search for the real meaning of death. I met many people and asked them about death. But each and every time I was getting disappointed because I didn't get what I expected. Then I read a lot of information about death. I watched many videos. I also read many novels.

One day, I read one thought. It is as follows -

"We have to live every day and to die one day." This sentence touched my heart and mind. I awoke and felt very positive at that time. The sentence touched me internally. Then I continued my further research on death.

I came to know many aspects of life - why we should live and how it is known to me actually. The things which I knew about death is: 'Death is nothing but a big misunderstanding among the people.' If you think of death, it is nothing but a change and a new beginning.

'Death is nothing but the new beginning and the biggest change within you.'

Let's understand with an example.

If you boil the water up to its boiling point, what will happen then? There won't be water in it. Does it mean that water died? No. It just converted into vapour, didn't it? If you cool it, it will be converted into water again.

Just think - what died during this process? The answer is 'nothing.' What did you see during this process? Yes. You see a change and transformation of energy

Death is nothing but a change in your life.

Nothing dies in this world and anything cannot be dead.

-Hrishikesh Tamkhane

What did you learn from this chapter?

www.ingramcontent.com/pod-product-compliance
Ingram Content Group UK Ltd.
Pitfield, Milton Keynes, MK11 3LW, UK
UKHW021935190726
13853UKWH00004B/1469